D1241224

A GARDEN BLESSING

A GARDEN

BLESSING

WELLERAN POLTARNEES

LAUGHING ELEPHANT BOOKS

YEAR MMIV 2004

LAUGHING ELEPHANT BOOKS

COPYRIGHT © 2000, BLUE LANTERN STUDIO

ISBN 1-883211-25-5

THIRD PRINTING   PRINTED IN SINGAPORE ALL RIGHTS RESERVED

LAUGHING ELEPHANT BOOKS

3645 INTERLAKE AVENUE NORTH   SEATTLE   98103

WWW.LAUGHINGELEPHANT.COM

COVER IMAGE: COLIN CAMPBELL COOPER (1856-1937). "PERGOLA AT SAMARKAND HOTEL," C.1921
OIL ON CANVAS, 29" X 36". COURTESY OF THE IRVINE MUSEUM, IRVINE, CALIFORNIA

I OFFER THIS BLESSING FOR YOU AND YOUR GARDEN, ENUMERATING THE MANY VIRTUES OF GARDENS THAT WE BE VIVIDLY AWARE OF THEIR PLACE IN OUR LIVES AND GRATEFUL FOR THEIR EXISTENCE.

WHEN YOU ENTER YOUR
GARDEN, LET IT BE AS
THOUGH YOU OPENED A
MAGIC GATE INTO A NEW
AND WONDERFUL WORLD–

A GARDEN BLESSING

A WORLD EVER CHANGING,

EVER NEW.

A GARDEN BLESSING

HERE ALL THE CARES OF
THE WORLD ARE
SHUT OUT, AND YOUR
CHALLENGES ARE
STRAIGHTFORWARD
AND IMMEDIATE.

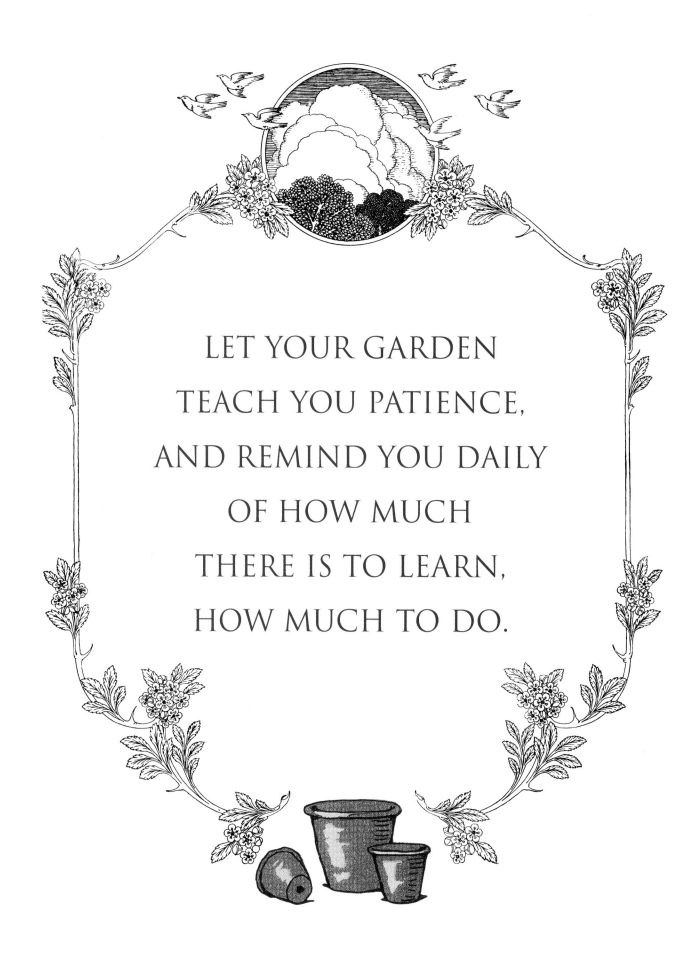

LET YOUR GARDEN
TEACH YOU PATIENCE,
AND REMIND YOU DAILY
OF HOW MUCH
THERE IS TO LEARN,
HOW MUCH TO DO.

A GARDEN BLESSING

MAY YOUR GARDEN
BE A PLACE WHERE
YOU CAN FIND PEACE –
WHERE TIME STANDS STILL.

LET YOUR GARDEN
REFRESH YOUR SENSES,
OPENING YOU
TO ITS MYRIAD
HUES AND SCENTS,

14

AND MAY IT ENCOURAGE
YOU TO LISTEN TO THE HUM
OF INSECTS, THE SONGS OF
THE BIRDS, THE SPLASH OF
WATER, AND THE SOUND OF
THE WIND THROUGH
THE TREES.

A GARDEN BLESSING

LET YOUR GARDEN
OFFER YOU, MANY TIMES
TO BE HAPPILY ALONE,

18

A GARDEN BLESSING

AND ALSO A PLACE FOR
CONVERSATION AND
BLOSSOMING FRIENDSHIPS.

A GARDEN BLESSING

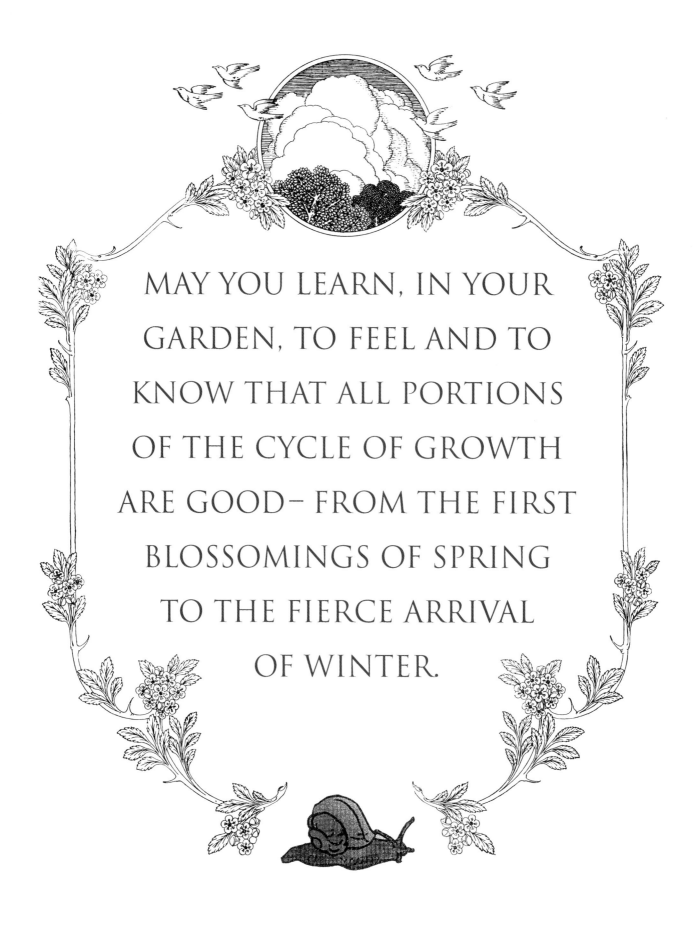

MAY YOU LEARN, IN YOUR
GARDEN, TO FEEL AND TO
KNOW THAT ALL PORTIONS
OF THE CYCLE OF GROWTH
ARE GOOD – FROM THE FIRST
BLOSSOMINGS OF SPRING
TO THE FIERCE ARRIVAL
OF WINTER.

A GARDEN BLESSING

I WISH FOR YOU SHADE AT
MIDDAY, AND ALSO PLACES
TO WARM YOURSELF
IN THE EARLY MORNINGS
AND LATE AFTERNOONS.

A GARDEN BLESSING

LET YOUR GARDEN
REACH OUT TO YOU
EVEN WITHIN YOUR HOME.

A GARDEN BLESSING

MAY IT FILL YOU WITH
THE WONDER OF NATURE'S
ENDLESS VARIETY, AND
THE POWERFUL FORCE OF
LIVING THINGS.

A GARDEN BLESSING

KNOW THAT YOUR GARDEN
IS A PLACE WHERE YOU
ARE NEEDED, WHERE YOUR
EFFORTS ARE VISIBLY
REWARDED, AND WHERE
NATURE COOPERATES
WITH YOUR WISHES.

A GARDEN BLESSING

LET THIS BE FOR YOU

A PLACE TO BE STILL

AND PEACEFUL.

A GARDEN BLESSING

35

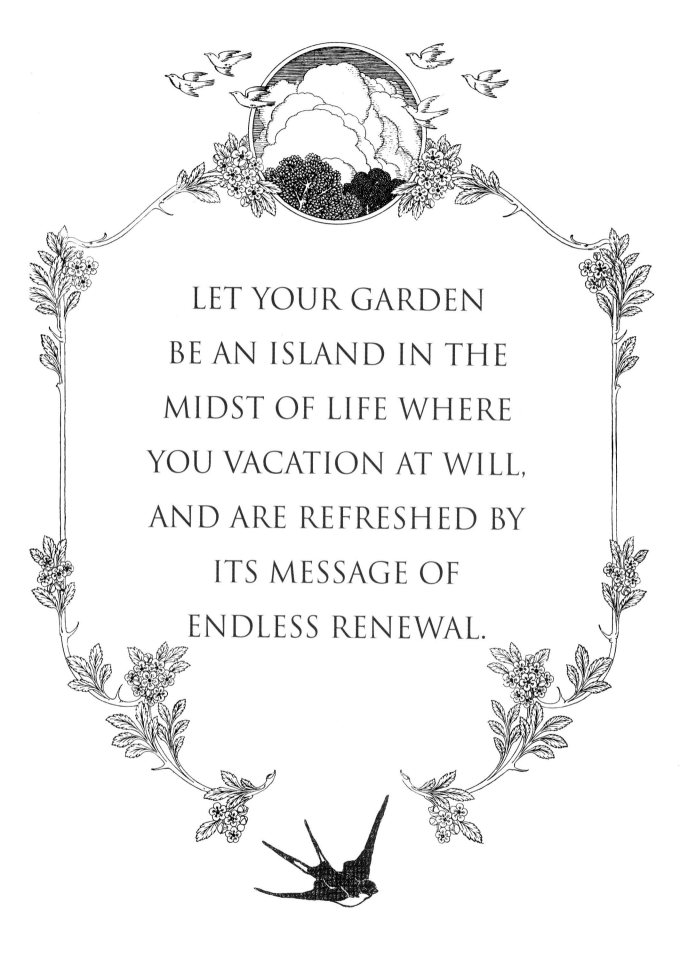

LET YOUR GARDEN
BE AN ISLAND IN THE
MIDST OF LIFE WHERE
YOU VACATION AT WILL,
AND ARE REFRESHED BY
ITS MESSAGE OF
ENDLESS RENEWAL.

A GARDEN BLESSING

37

KNOW THAT THE
LIFE YOU HAVE GIVEN
TO YOUR GARDEN,
YOUR GARDEN WILL
GIVE BACK TO YOU.

A GARDEN BLESSING

39

PICTURE CREDITS

Cover	Colin Campbell Cooper (1856-1937). "Pergola at Samarkand Hotel," c.1921 oil on canvas, 29" x 36". Courtesy of the Irvine Museum, Irvine, California
Endpapers	George S. Elgood. "Ramscliffe: Orange Lilies & Monkshood," 1898.
Halftitle	Unknown. Magazine cover, 1932
Title page	Unknown. Advertising art, 1917.
Frontispiece	Childe Hassam. "Geraniums," 1888.
Copyright +42	T.M. Cleland. Title page decoration for garden book, 1904.
ix	F.C. Frieseke. "Hollyhocks," 1914.
x	Claude Monet. "Le Jardin de L'artiste à Giverny," 1900.
1	Franklin Booth. Border design, 1918.
3	Unknown. Magazine cover, 1925.
5	Max Kuehne. "View of the Garden," n.d.
7	Diego Rivera. "En el Viñedo," 1920.
9	Laurits Tuxen. "Rhododendron in the garden at the Artist's villa 'Dagminne' in Skagen," 1917.
11	Suzanne Valadon. "Les Jardins de la Rue Cortot," 1922.
12/13	Theodore Wores. "My Studio Home in Saratoga," 1926.
15	Childe Hassam. "Isles of Shoals Garden," 1892.
17	Margaret Fisher Prout. "The Fountain," n.d.
19	Edward Dufner. "Morning Sunshine," c. 1925.
21	Henri-Joseph Lebasque. "Cueillant des Fleurs," 1923.
23	Frederick Walker. "Autumn," 1865.
25	William Glackens. "Garden at Hartford," 1918.
27	Richard Miller. "Morning Sunlight," c. 1914.
29	Grace Sainsbury. "Telling the Time," 1895.
30/31	Henri-Jean-Guillaume Martin. "Fountain and Flower," n.d.
33	Ritold Gordon. Magazine cover, 1931.
35	Oscar Bluhm. "In the Pergola," 1892.
37	Daniel Ridgway Knight. "Woman in a Garden," n.d.
39	C.W.R. Magazine cover, 1904.
41	Frank Bramley. "Delicious Solitude," 1909.
43	B.B. Bains. Magazine cover, 1927.

Garden decorations from the *The Garden*, circa 1900 are used on the following pages:
2, 4, 6, 8, 10, 14, 16, 18, 20, 22, 24, 26, 28, 32, 34, 36, and 38

COLOPHON

BOOK DESIGN: SACHEVERELL DARLING AT BLUE LANTERN STUDIO

TYPESET IN TRAJAN & CASLON

PRINTED BY STAR STANDARD